"*You can't defeat the darkness by keeping it caged inside of you.*"

Seth Adam Smith

freebird

by Laura Muensterer

Kelley Creative
Rowlett, Texas, USA

An earlier edition of this book was published in 2018 by Laura Muensterer.

ISBNs: 978-1-7331088-9-8 Hardback
978-1-7331088-7-4 Paperback
978-1-7331088-8-1 eBook

All rights reserved. Published by Kelley Creative.
www.kelleycreative.design

Cover artwork by Nicole Scherer.
www.ellehell.com
The text type was set in Gabriola.

MUSINGS

1

life

[[*illuminate*]]

Think back
To when you were young
Full of light and laughter

Why did everything suddenly change
And the world become so dark

Whatever you do
Don't let the darkness consume you

Instead
Choose to be the light

Because
I have seen the darkness

And everyone deserves
To have someone

Turn the light back on

←*l.n.m.*→

[[*destiny*]]

Lines crossed
Sense of self lost

No definite way to travel
No light at the end of the tunnel

Right
Left
Straight
Across

Which path will you take
To start a clean slate

Maybe
As long as it's your decision
It will become

Everything you've envisioned

← *l.n.m.* →

[[*existence*]]

Do you ever feel
The weight of the world
Resting underneath your tired eyes

Every time you blink
You get this tinge of pain
That travels up your spine

"I'm just tired"
You say

As you wipe away your makeup
Pull on your pajamas
Turn off the light

And pretend everything's alright

←—*l.n.m.*—→

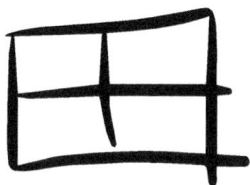

[[*drive*]]

Hands on the wheel
Foot on the gas

There's nowhere to go
But forward

Windows rolled down
Hair in your face
Music blasting

There are no thoughts
Emotions
Or fears

Just nameless faces
Stacks of concrete at every corner

And windows into the unknown

↞ *l.n.m.* ↠

[[metamorphosis]]

We often think
In order to succeed in life
We must never experience

Pain
Sadness
Or failure

But the only way
We can grow and thrive
Is if we experience
These terrible things

For it is only in these moments
We take a hard look at our life

Whether or not
We're going in the direction
Our heart and soul desire

Just as a butterfly must shed its cocoon
We too must shed our past selves

And lose the layers
That are no longer aiding

In our own personal evolution

←*l.n.m.*→

[[*discovery*]]

Turning a book's pages
Is a lot like life

So many words and experiences
Washed away
By one single flip of paper

Feel the page
The sharpness of its edges
Cutting through days of old emotions

Digging a hole
Deep in your soul
Only to uncover a wound

That you never noticed before

←*l.n.m.*→

⟦ *foolish* ⟧

The thought
Of this being my new normal
My new standard of living

Brings me to think
About all the times
I was tired of my routine

How silly was I
To push comfort away
As if it had done me wrong

And welcome in unfamiliarity

With nothing but my wide open arms

«— *l.n.m.* —»

[[*perspective*]]

If you separate yourself
From the screen

You'll soon realize
That your grass

Is actually quite green

« *l.n.m.* »

[[*obstacles*]]

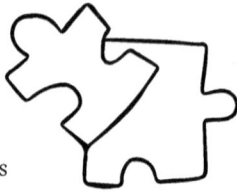

The puzzles of our lives
Rarely form
Without some kind of twisted storm

It rips through our comfort zone
To see if we can truly make it

All on our own

⟵ *l.n.m.* ⟶

Do you ever look out the window
Just to appreciate the sunset

Do you ever step outside
And let the smell
Of fresh green grass fill the air

Some days I lose track
Of these little intricacies

The details of life
The beauty of nature

The birds chirping in the trees
The kids playing in the leaves

Listen to the sounds
Of this world

They are our only small moments of simplicity

↞ *l.n.m.* ↠

[[*hope*]]

The path I was following
That was supposed to lead me somewhere

One day ended
Without any notice

But then
Months later

I mowed away all the grass and the leaves
Uncovered all of the trees

And before I knew it

I finally felt a breeze

← *l.n.m.* →

[[*choice*]]

Remember darling
The world is your canvas

You can either choose to be at war
Or you can make the conscious decision

To go out and explore

←← *l.n.m.* →→

[[*disconnected*]]

I think back
To when I was a kid

And had a million things
I wanted to achieve

But then
School started wearing me down

Homework
Tests
And projects

Made me want to drown
Until the child in me

No longer wanted to come around

← *l.n.m.* →

[*adulthood*]

Storytime
Used to be a lot of fun

Until
Everyone's stories

Became a lot more glum

← *l.n.m.* →

[[*blossom*]]

Every time I travel
I feel like I'm on top of the world

No matter where I go

It's always a new chance to grow

← *l.n.m.* →

[[*gratitude*]]

Every day
I drag myself out of bed

And tell myself
To make the most of the day

Every day
It gets a little harder

All I want to do
Is stay in the shower

But then
I realize
I have the best job in the world

Not necessarily because of what I do
But because every day

I get to experience something new

« *l.n.m.* »

[[*uncertainty*]]

I always dreamed
Of being on my own
But now

The dream has cleared
Reality has shifted
The sleepy fog has been lifted

No one shows me where to go
Or what I should do

All I want
Is an instruction booklet

Telling me my next move

←*l.n.m.*→

[[*bliss*]]

There is something
So calming
About the sea

Waves crashing beneath you
Sand getting stuck between your toes
The wind tickling your nose

There is no screen or glass
Blocking your view

You're simply enjoying

Everything that makes up you

← *l.n.m.* →

[[evolution]]

Growing up
Is a lot like sharpening a pencil

Every so often
Your tip gets dull

Until one day
You're sharpened again

Maybe through a pat on your back
Or an unexpected compliment

You start writing your story once more
Filling each page with experiences and wonder

Passion for life
And all it has to offer

You find the angles you like
The ones that hit your desires just right

And then
The cycle repeats itself

Over and over again
Until you've regrown so many times
Your story ends

Allowing you to finally make amends

← *l.n.m.* →

[[*fog*]]

There used to be
So much creativity in me

Oozing its way out
Begging to be free

But then
Adult responsibilities
Clouded up

All of my artistic energy

←*l.n.m.*→

II

time

[[*change*]]

People you always thought would be there
Suddenly feel distant

Places you swore you'd never leave
No longer feel like home

Memories you once held so dearly

Give way to moments you never thought you'd know

←← *l.n.m.* →→

[[*absent*]]

As you grow older
You become emotionless

Moving through the motions
While failing to appreciate

The present moment

←*l.n.m.*→

[[*longing*]]

You grow up thinking
As soon as you're an adult
Everything will come together perfectly

But then
As the years go on

You start to pick up on things
You never noticed before

Stuff like heartbreak
Betrayal
And disappointment

Become part of your daily life
Making you wish

You could go back
To when you were a child

Oblivious to the evils of the world
Filled with hope for the future
And having every reason to believe

The good ones will never leave

← *l. n. m.* →

[[*haven*]]

As we grow older
Our definition of home changes

It starts out
As a safe place
With our parents

But then
Gradually grows into
A place without any walls or floors

Maybe home is a person
Or simply a state of mind

My home remains inside of me
But sometimes

I wish I could go back
To when I had no concerns

And a safe place for my mind to return

← *l.n.m.* →

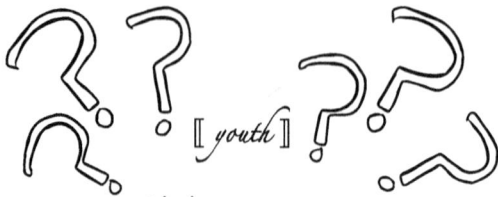

[[*youth*]]

I look into your eyes
And see parts of myself in you

I wonder how much misery you have faced
How many tears you have cried

Will I grow to have your wrinkles
And sunspots on my skin

When I sit and watch children
Who are as careless as can be

I remember there's only so much time left
Until I'm sitting across the table
And faced with these silly questions

But then
I look into your eyes
And wonder once more

Maybe these questions aren't all that silly after all

↞ *l.n.m.* ↠

⟦ *euphoria* ⟧

When summer comes
And winter waves goodbye

Our hearts return
To the days of climbing trees
While shooing away bees

Oh how wonderful
Those moments were
That we constantly took for granted

Thinking we had
An infinite amount of time

To live life so enchanted

← *l.n.m.* →

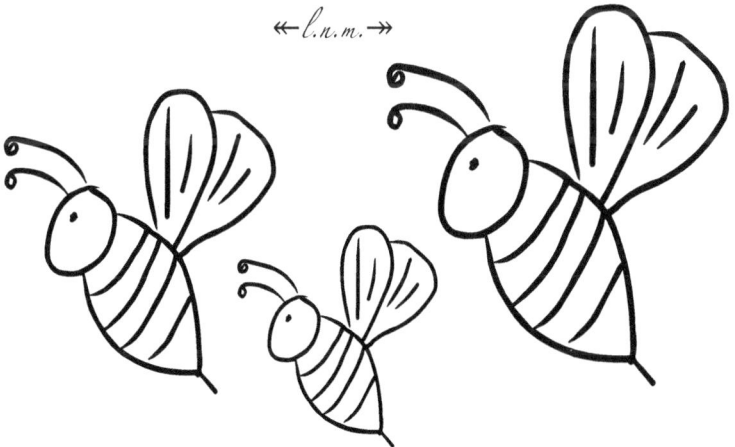

[[*groundwork*]]

I have always found myself
Living too much in the future

Staying in the present moment
Has never been my strength

But
I try my best to stop worrying
And start living

Because
No matter how much
We try to plan ahead

All we can do
Is make the present moment

A solid foundation for our future

← *l. n. m.* →

[[*nostalgia*]]

We live in a world
Surrounded by photographs

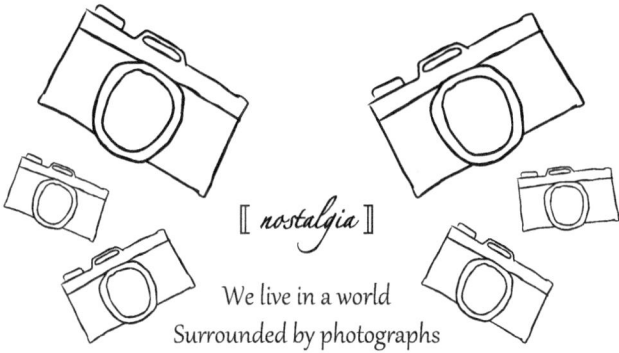

Little moments of time
Reminding us of all the experiences
We'd do anything to relive again

Peer into their faces
Look into their souls

What's hidden underneath
The small creases in their skin
The tension right below their chin

What about their watery eyes
Hiding tears and little lies

About to burst and reveal
Fear that there will never be

A moment as wonderful as this again

← *l.n.m.* →

[[*phantom*]]

Time is constantly haunting us
Making us feel like we're running out
Of something that's imagined

Will you give in
To its intimidation

Or decide
To look the other way

Will you take life
Like a grain of sand

Each particle unique
Carrying its own purpose

Maybe it's there to help you grow
Or maybe it's there to show you

Just how far you have to go

« *l.n.m.* »

[[alive]]

Look at the sky
Has it always been this blue

Peer down to the water
Has it always felt this smooth

There are only so many years left
Until we'll return to the stars

And simply admire

All of these things from afar

«*l.n.m.*»

Remember when we used to climb so high
We felt like we could touch the sky

Those blissful moments of youth
Quickly disappeared as age took over

But no matter how much time passes
No matter how far we are from each other

We still have the sky
The trees
And the leaves

Reminding us
Of those beautiful days of youth

When we thought all we knew

Was the truth

←*l.n.m.*→

[[*drifting*]]

When you're a kid
You think everyone around you
Knows what they're doing

But then
You grow up and realize

Everyone's just making it up
As they go along

There is no path or right way
We're all just fish

Swimming in a sea of uncertainty

←— *l.n.m.* —→

[[*presence*]]

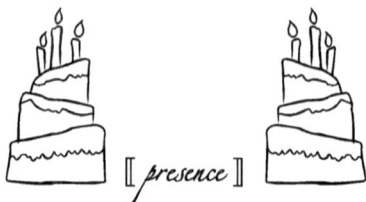

As we grow older
Birthdays become less about presents

And more about being present

←← *l.n.m.* →→

[[*finale*]]

Life is so fragile
Yet we live as if
We're a cat with nine lives

When it comes down to it
We're just specks in the universe

Floating through life
Assuming we have all the time in the world

When in reality
The minute we opened our eyes

A clock began ticking
Counting down the days

Until we part our ways

↞ *l.n.m.* ↠

[[*lost*]]

There are so many moments
I would do anything
To experience again

They always disappear
From my memory

Before I can absorb

Every detail again

«*l.n.m.*»

[[*stubborn*]]

Take a step back
And look through the years

Are you proud of what you've done
Are you happy with what you've said

When you're old and sickly
Praying for the sweet kiss of death

Will you feel good about your life
Or will you be filled with regret

At the end of the day
All we really are is trees

Growing roots

And evolving as we please

« *l.n.m.* »

III

humanity

[[*windows*]]

Look into people's eyes
What do you see

Are there sprinkles of hope
Spottings of sadness

As you grow older
You begin to realize

We hold so many stories

In those small little spaces

«— *l. n. m.* —»

[[*human*]]

On the outside
I'm an adult

I go to my job
Come home

Make dinner
Sleep
Repeat

But on the inside
All I want

Is somebody's hand to hold

← *l.n.m.* →

[[*phases*]]

We're a lot like the weather
We all have our seasons
Our own individual temperatures

Hot
Cold
Humid
Dry

Some days we're rainy
Other days we're full of sun

Maybe today there's a drizzle

Maybe tomorrow there's a tornado

« *l.n.m.* »

[[*detached*]]

Everything from our dating habits
To the way we treat our parents

Makes up the culture
We live in today

I often think about
The way of life we've created
And I wonder if it makes me proud

Is this what we had in mind

Or are we all simply blind

≪ *l.n.m.* ≫

[[*lifetime*]]

So many women
Grow up hating their skin
And all of the wrinkles within

But in many ways
Wrinkles are badges of honor

Commending a job well done
In this thing called life

That ages us
And sucks up our youth

Forcing us to discover our innermost truth

←*l.n.m.*→

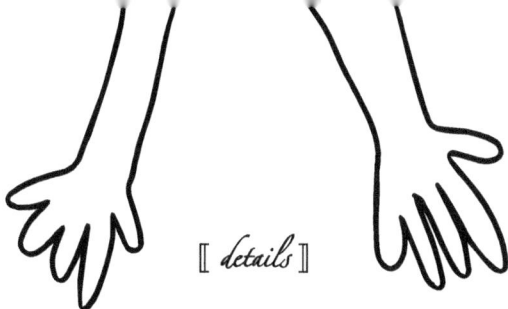

[[*details*]]

They say the eyes are the windows to the soul
But what about fingers and hands

Look at their nails
Are they perfectly trimmed and aligned
Or are they ragged and uneven

Are there hangnails around the edges
Bite marks from everyday stress

Nails painted in pastels
Or bright and bold
With subtle speckles of gold

From our hands to our fingers
We all have stories
Hidden in the cracks and creases of our skin

Reminding us of all the battles

We are silently fighting within

← *l.n.m.* →

[[*regret*]]

How many mistakes will it take
Before we realize
We are our own worst enemy

We love to point our fingers
And place the blame on someone else

But at the end of the day
We are the ones with the blood on our hands
Patiently waiting for someone to understand

That we are not running away from people
Places
Or responsibilities

But rather the ghost of what once was

Infinite possibility

« *l.n.m.* »

[[*confusion*]]

We're all a little stained in some way
Our view is never quite clear

Once our glass is smeared

It's hard to find the right way to steer

«— *l.n.m.* —»

[[*envy*]]

I've always been fascinated by children
Their minds are so

Open
Honest
And carefree

They simply do what they please
Even if it means they'll end up

With a scraped knee

«―*l.n.m.*―»

[[*delusion*]]

What secrets are you hiding
Far away from your senses
Locked away from reality

These secrets are slowly killing you
Eating away at your mind and body

Waiting for you to come to the realization
That until you tell yourself the truth
You'll constantly be hiding your true soul

Everything that makes your heart full

« *l.n.m.* »

[[*empowered*]]

One day
I realized my whole life has been different
Because I'm a girl

I look back on certain situations
And wonder if they would've had a happier ending
If I had been on the opposite side

Regardless of these outcomes
I like being a girl

Some days my mind eats me alive
While other times I find

Every reason to strive

← l.n.m. →

[[*hooked*]]

A person
Is like a ship

If there is nothing
Anchoring them down

They will simply drown

↞ *l.n.m.* ↠

I have made it a habit
To avoid the news

When I was younger
My mind could forget
All of the gory details

But now
I internalize everything

Every shooting
Injustice
And horror

Seeps into my skin
Reminding me

That we're all secretly evil within

← *l.n.m.* →

54

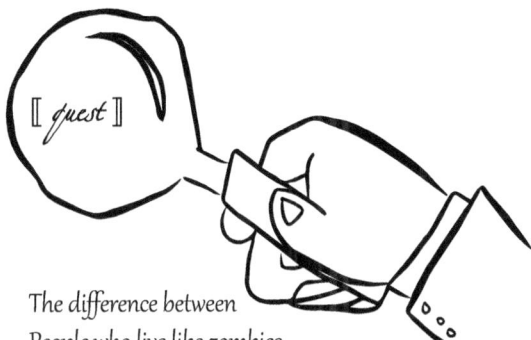

[[quest]]

The difference between
People who live like zombies
And those who experience life fully

Is that some of us
Hold on to our secrets

While the rest of us
Accept our fate
And spend the majority of our lives

Searching for anyone else who can relate

«‑ *l.n.m.* ‑»

[[*buried*]]

When we're reckless kids
We have our parents
To piece us back together

But then we grow up
And are forced to learn
Which piece goes where

I'm still figuring out the puzzle
There are many pieces I have yet to discover

But I know they're in me somewhere

Hidden deep in my despair

«— *l.n.m.* —»

[[*harmony*]]

Humans are complicated beings
One day we're high
And the next day we're low

I will be an accomplished person
The day I finally find balance

Between work
Love
And friendship

Not too little of anything
Not too much of anything

Everything in my life

Fits exactly just right

←*l.n.m.*→

IV

relationships

[[idle]]

Real love
Has slowly been taken over by online dating

Creating a world
Where people are interested in anything

But relating

≪ *l.n.m.* ≫

[[*liberation*]]

Back and forth
Up and down

Learning and growing
As one

But then one day
Things just aren't the same

The clouds start calling your name
Asking you to come play a game

So you let go of his hand
And go learn for yourself
How to reach the sky

While finding your own way to fly

⟪ *l.n.m.* ⟫

[[*naivety*]]

When we were children
We played together for the last time
Without even realizing it

Years pass us by
And eventually
Play is replaced with pain

We navigate it step by step
Sometimes in the same space
Other times light years away

We reunite for days
Months
Or even years

And then one day
We reach the end of our journey

The goodbye is implied
But nobody knows it

Except the sky

←*l.n.m.*→

[[*foreigner*]]

After a certain age
I could no longer relate to my peers

I felt out of place and out of touch
Grasping for a sense of belonging
All too much

But over time
I've started to accept
I will never be like them

In many ways
You could consider me an alien

Placed on this earth
As some kind of sick joke

But at the end of the day
The joke is on them

Because now that I'm older
It's gotten easier to blend in

As if I'm some sort of chameleon

←*l.n.m.*→

The beauty of relationships
Is that you get to choose
Whether or not you become

Allies
Or enemies

Some people seem to think
Being enemies is the worst thing
In the world

But
With certain relationships

Not being allies
Is the best thing

Life can ever bring

← *l.n.m.* →

[[*stranger*]]

Trust is a tricky thing
It takes years to build up
And only one minute to destroy

Maybe you are the one
Who has lost trust

Or maybe they are the one
Who has done you wrong

Suddenly those familiar eyes
Once filled with love and memories

Are now encased

In the body of an enemy

← *l.n.m.* →

[[*temporary*]]

Many times the cure of sadness
Can be found in the kiss of their lips
The love in their eyes

When they gently touch your skin
Whisper in your ear
And transport you to a cloud of oblivion

Blissfully oblivious
To your own problems

Ignorant of all
The stress that lies ahead

Silencing the voices in your head
Blocking all the harmful tendencies you so often dread
Allowing you to be at peace instead

For just a few moments
It's simply you and them
Floating through the sky

Patiently waiting
Until the next time

The sun says its goodbye

← *l.n.m.* →

[[*contact*]]

We often forget how healing
A simple touch can be

Think about the last time
You gave someone a hug
Or a pat on the shoulder

Do you remember
The release you both felt

Do you miss the feeling

Of being so close

«—*l.n.m.*—»

⟦ *dead end* ⟧

When you're a healer
You naturally attract people

With dark pasts

And happiness that never lasts

≪—*l. n. m.*—≫

[[*mindset*]]

Many of the problems
We face daily

Can be traced back to one moment
One memory of pain

That completely changed the trajectory
Of our life plan

We spend our adulthood
Reliving these situations
And replaying old patterns

Constantly questioning the things
That have happened to us

When really
All it takes

Is a little self-reflection
To stop these habits in their track
And create a new direction

For our own limitless progression

← *l.n.m.* →

[[*fulfilled*]]

There are so many frogs
You will kiss and regret

Before you finally find a man
Who will teach you

There is no fairytale
And that real love

Exists after all

← *l.n.m.* →

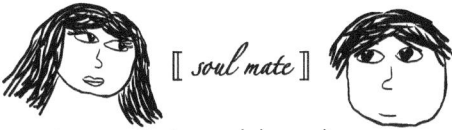

[[*soul mate*]]

Society and the media
Have brainwashed us to think
That in order to be in love

You must be an amazing match
A perfect pair

But the beauty of a spouse
Is not in their similarity to you

But rather in the fact that they see through
Other people's limited points of view
And create a brand-new way

Of looking at you

« *l.n.m.* »

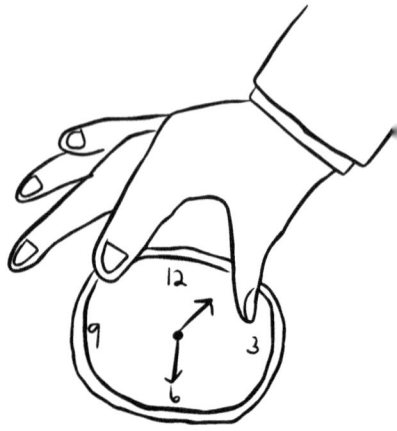

[[*used*]]

If you give away
Your time and energy

Without expecting
Anything in return

People will eventually

Stop giving you the time of day

←*l.n.m.*→

[[naked]]

Intimacy
Can be a scary thing

Especially when you've trained yourself

To hold it all in

≪ *l.n.m.* ≫

V

mind

[[*willpower*]]

When we're young
Our minds are open

But as we grow older
Fences are born

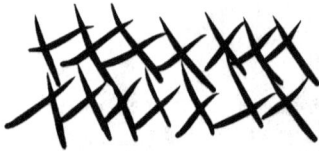

They trap us
Confine us

Little do we know
Our sharpest spike
Is there to guide us

And grow us
To our full potential

Will you let the fences
Poke holes in your might
Or will you use them

To go against the tide of your mind

⟵ l.n.m. ⟶

[[*trapped*]]

No one else has to live
In your mind

No one else
Has to feel your

Pain
Sadness
Or tears

Because of this
We cannot let anyone tell us

How to think
Feel
Or act

Because
At the end of the day

We are the ones

Who are forced to stay

←*l.n.m.*→

77

[[*tendencies*]]

Sometimes
You have to dig a hole
Deep inside your soul

To uncover all of the habits and patterns
Creating cycles of confusion

I have many habits I try to break
In my obsession with perfection

If I can just track down that first mistake
Maybe I can prevent myself from getting lost
In all of the endless repetition

The cycle will break
And I will recenter
Back into the real world

Where my happiness can reenter

←*l.n.m.*→

[[*stranded*]]

My emotions are like the waves
Some days they bring me to new places
Where I get to know new faces

And other times they return me
To my own private island

Where all I'm left with
Is hopeless concern

And a pretty terrible sunburn

←*l.n.m.*→

[[*open-minded*]]

I want to make sure
The way I experience life
Isn't muddied with unrealistic world views

Because every person has their own story
Struggles
And perspectives

Collected through various wins
And losses

That merge to create a whole new way
Of looking at things

Giving outsiders wings
To fly into new dimensions of thought
And see just how much

Pain and pleasure have brought

←*l.n.m.*→

[[*infinite*]]

My mind is a galaxy

It lives in the universe

«— *l.n.m.* —»

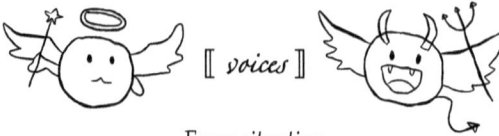

[[*voices*]]

Every situation
Has its own ending

Sometimes
We lead the way

Other times
Our ego

Gets in the way

← *l.n.m.* →

[[*instinct*]]

Being introverted is confusing
Sometimes you enjoy
Spending time with others

And other times
You find your mind
Telling you to stay

Tucked deep inside

«—*l.n.m.*—»

Time flies
When you're floating
Through the sky

Enjoying those glorious moments
Of closing your eyes
And escaping the everyday

No noise
No distractions

Just you and your mind
In a dream-world of thoughts

Journeying through your desires
While being reminded of all the times

You've never felt higher

⇐ l.n.m. ⇛

[[*occupied*]]

Anxiety is like another person
Living in your mind

Cluttering up your rooms and floors
Even though the space is supposed to be

All yours

«— *l.n.m.* —»

[[*noise*]]

Thoughts constantly knock on the door
Asking if I can listen a bit more

Kicking and demanding recognition

Of anything but my intuition

↞ *l.n.m.* ↠

[[*purify*]]

Peer into your mind
What do you see

Hope
Fear
Regret

Maybe happiness is hiding in a corner
Begging you not to be a foreigner

Maybe loathing is hiding behind a wall
Hoping to cause your next downfall

Whatever is living in your mind
Remember to do some spring cleaning
Every once in awhile

To get rid of all the hate

So you can finally see straight

←*l.n.m.*→

[[oxygen]]

One day
I decided I didn't want to fight
With my mind anymore

It had become a constant battle
I was no longer winning

Once you lose control of your thoughts
It's as if your whole soul has sunken

Left deep down in the sea
With no air to breathe

But
Once you make the decision
To befriend your mind

Suddenly
You come up for air

The sun hits your skin
You lift up your chin

And let out the biggest grin

«—l.n.m.—»

88

[[*unstable*]]

Do you ever unravel
Bit by bit
Piece by piece

Some strands short
Others tall

They fall before

You can catch them all

↞ *l.n.m.* ↠

[[*ambush*]]

I have had anxiety
Ever since I can remember

I never realized it was anxiety
I simply thought this was how everyone felt

Mind filled with endless questions and worries
Preventing you from ever feeling a sense of security

Now that I know what anxiety is
I try my very hardest to fight back

And take a stand against every attack

← *l.n.m.* →

⟦ *fear* ⟧

I can feel dependency
Creeping up on me

Touching the shoulder
Of my independence

And whispering in its ear
That if it needs anything

Dependency is always here

←—*l.n.m.*—→

[[*purge*]]

When we're born
Our minds are squeaky clean

All we have
Is our instincts

But as we grow older
Our minds are filled with trash

It clutters our worldview
And makes us quite literally
Lose ourselves

I'm taking the trash out
Day by day

Picking up the small pieces
So that eventually

My mind is as clear as the first day

«― *l.n.m.* ―»

[[*busy*]]

If you view anxiety as a roadblock
As opposed to a wall

It gets easier

To ignore its calls

« *l.n.m.* »

[[*paranoia*]]

I feel like I'm constantly racing the clock
Inching my way to a finish line
That doesn't actually exist

The end destination is all in my mind

Leaving all of my real goals and desires behind

←← *l.n.m.* →→

[[*broken*]]

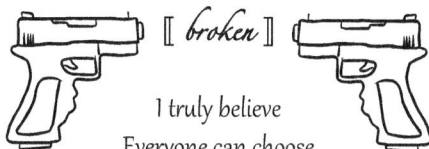

I truly believe
Everyone can choose

To be more aware
Of their surroundings

Or forever ignorant
Regardless of the cost to humanity

But for some
There is no choice

Suddenly
A world of perspectives is opened
And your soul is dragged into an endless black hole

Of evil
Deceit
And disappointment

There are no more unicorns and rainbows
Just a void of disgust and disarray
Destroying everything familiar

Homes are now filled with villains
Forests reek of carnage
And once safe spaces

Carry memories of mass murder

↞ *l.n.m.* ↠

[[*expectations*]]

The ego has a way
Of tricking us into ill intentions

Making us question
Every little suggestion

Analyzing it
For any possible hint of deception

When in many ways
All we really crave

Is our own version of perfection

←*l.n.m.*→

[[*possibilities*]]

What if you're not actually missing out
On your next big moment

Your next grand entrance
Into the sweet feeling of success

What if the future is not actually empty
But rather filled to the brim
With unlimited dreams and potential

Only you can uncover it
Only you can push desperation away

Deep into the shadows
Far away from your consciousness

Leaving the voices inside of you
To come to the inevitable realization
That desperation was never your friend

It was only ever a meaningless distraction

From your next brilliant plan of action

←*l.n.m.*→

VI

self-love

[[*rebirth*]]

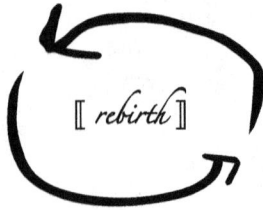

Once I took back control over
The pieces of my body

I stopped looking for people
To replace the holes in my heart

Now my heart is filled
With a bunch of beautiful art

Giving me the chance to restart
So the pieces that make up me

Never again have to fall apart

← *l.n.m.* →

⟦ *myth* ⟧

Perfection is an intangible thing
None of us can ever really achieve

We often draw a picture
In our minds

Of what perfection looks like
Feels like
And acts like

But at the end of the day
Nothing is quite as perfect

As they all say

↞ *l.n.m.* ↠

[[outlook]]

Aging can be the most amazing experience
Or it can take you by the belt loop
And twist your pants all up into a knot

Making every move uncomfortable
Every step unbearable

But when you choose to let age happen
And appreciate all of the value it brings

Instead of regretting the past
You'll look forward to the future

Because you'll now understand
That underneath all of the flaws

You'll find beauty in it all

« *l.n.m.* »

⟦ *important* ⟧

Breathe in
Breathe out

Feel your chest
Feel your heart

You are a growing being
Filled with a million tiny particles

Constantly flowing
So that you can

Continue glowing

↞ *l.n.m.* ↠

[[*flawed*]]

What if
Instead of trying to cover up
All of our cracks

We honor the things
That make us unique

Every imperfect square
Every twisted triangle

Is the secret recipe

To our own survival

← *l.n.m.* →

[[*confidence*]]

I have been knocked down
Far more times
Than I have been lifted up

But I do not view this
As a problem at all

In fact
It has trained me

To always stand tall

←*l.n.m.*→

[[*answer*]]

So many people grow up thinking
It's what's on the outside that matters

But I have felt ugly
And I have felt beautiful

And no matter what I look like that day
I always feel the most beautiful
When I am in control of my mind

When there's no one to answer to
But my own whims and desires

I decide whether or not I'm beautiful
I hold the key to everything

That makes up me

←*l.n.m.*→

[[*worthy*]]

Imagine if every hair
That fell off your head

Was your stress
Doubts
And fears
Disappearing forever

Leaving no more gloom
Just more room

For all of the good things to bloom

←*l.n.m.*→

[[*therapy*]]

Space
Is so important

Oftentimes
We forget

How healing it can be
To simply enjoy

Our own company

«— *l.n.m.* —»

[[*perception*]]

When people belittle me
And act as if I carry no worth

I try to focus less on the flaws within myself
And more on the problems they're most likely facing

Deep inside their mind
Where happiness has been left behind

Making room for more self-hatred and depression

Leaving nothing but twisted impressions

←*l.n.m.*→

[[*complete*]]

Once you start
Truly loving yourself

Your hair
Finally grows

Your skin
Finally clears

But the greatest growth
Is in your mind

It no longer bullies you
Into insanity

Instead
It values your point of view

Allowing you to completely renew

«—*l.n.m.*—»

[[*concept*]]

The way people see you
Is so different
From how you view yourself

There are a thousand perceptions of you
Based on your ideas
Feelings
And actions

Anytime you worry about your image
Remember
You're not just somebody living one life

But rather a person
Of many different lives

It all just depends on the eyes

← *l.n.m.* →

Thank you

For taking the time to travel
Into the depths of my mind

For being kind
Patient
And maybe even a little understanding

I hope these words
Have helped heal your wounds
Like they've helped heal mine

XOXO
Laura

About the Author

Laura Muensterer is an avid writer who uses creative storytelling to express her innermost thoughts, emotions and fears about the world. Through poetry and illustration, Laura explores various aspects of the human experience while shedding light on the many ways our past shapes our present and future self.

After obtaining her bachelor's degree in public relations, Laura worked in the marketing industry for a few years, where she specialized in social media and copywriting. During this time, she self-published her first book, *freebird*, on Amazon. Post-publication, she pursued certification as a life coach while continuing to publish new poetry on her Instagram page, *@afreebirdflies*.

In addition to writing poetry, Laura hosts a podcast titled *freebird radio*. A self-proclaimed foodie, she loves to try cuisine from many cultures, which goes hand-in-hand with her love for international travel. Born in Germany, Laura lived in Texas for 15 years before relocating to San Diego, California. A true Texan, she loves to ride horses and enjoy the simpler things in life.

www.ingramcontent.com/pod-product-compliance
Lightning Source LLC
Chambersburg PA
CBHW071601040426
42452CB00008B/1253